Kisho Kurokawa
Nakagin Capsule Tower

EVANGELOS KOTSIORIS

THE MUSEUM OF MODERN ART, NEW YORK

Kisho Kurokawa Architect & Associates (Japan, est. 1962). Capsule A1305 from the Nakagin Capsule Tower. 1970–72; restored 2022–23. Steel, wood, paint, plastics, cloth, polyurethane, glass, ceramic, and electronics, 8′ 4 ⅜″ × 8′ 10 ⁵⁄₁₆″ × 13′ 10 ⁹⁄₁₆″ (255 × 270 × 423 cm). THE MUSEUM OF MODERN ART, NEW YORK. GIFT OF JO CAROLE AND RONALD S. LAUDER, ALICE AND TOM TISCH, AND THE NAKAGIN CAPSULE TOWER PRESERVATION AND RESTORATION PROJECT, TOKYO

"THIS BUILDING IS NOT AN APARTMENT HOUSE," DECLARED THE JAPANESE ARCHITECT Kisho Kurokawa in the first sentence of a statement about his office's design for the Nakagin Capsule Tower building, completed in Tokyo between 1970 and 1972 **[FIG. 1]**.[1] This unusual emphasis on what a building was *not* signaled that what looked like a peculiar housing structure was in fact something much more—a pioneering experiment in urban living. Consisting of 140 single-occupancy "capsules" attached to two concrete-and-steel towers, the building offered businessmen a compact pied-à-terre so that they could spend the night in Tokyo's vibrant Ginza district after a long day's work instead of returning to their homes in dormitory towns. On a technical level, the Nakagin Capsule Tower also pushed the boundaries of prefabricating architecture. Its living units were constructed almost entirely in a factory, then transported to the site, lifted by crane, and each one secured in place with four high-tension bolts. Measuring no larger than a one- to two-person travel trailer, each capsule came equipped with an en suite bathroom, built-in bed, foldout desk, telephone, and color TV **[FIG. 2]**. Because of their small footprint, the capsules created an intimate interior in the sky, while their distinctive circular windows framed dynamic city views—from the streaks of car lights on the elevated expressway nearby to Tokyo Bay in the distance and, on clear days, even the snow-capped peak of Mount Fuji. A hybrid of a hotel, a condominium, and a business center, Kurokawa's building suggested a new type of urban infrastructure for Japan's nomadic office workers.

Since its inception in the late 1960s, the Nakagin Capsule Tower has come to be one of the most discussed and written-about modern buildings of the twentieth century. A groundbreaking proposition for how architecture could radically reshape the way we inhabit cities in the future, Kurokawa's design has been the object of countless articles, books, and documentaries, as well as a prominent feature in architecture exhibitions, including three at The Museum of Modern Art in New York.[2] After more than fifty years of continuous occupation, a contested history of limited maintenance, and multiple attempts to secure its restoration and preservation, the building ultimately had to be disassembled in the summer of 2022. Even though the Nakagin Capsule Tower no longer stands, the ideas that gave birth to it live on. The building and the provocative ideas behind it continue to inspire new generations of architects and wider audiences alike to ask questions about how we can live together in urban settings.

Kisho Kurokawa Architect & Associates (Japan, est. 1962). Nakagin Capsule Tower, Tokyo. 1970–72. Exterior view. 1972. Photograph: Tomio Ohashi

FIG. 1. Kisho Kurokawa in one of the Nakagin Capsule Tower units, c. 1972

For Kurokawa, the design was a physical amalgamation of a diverse range of ideas, from his observations on the changing nature of Japanese living culture to contemporary mobility and the overwhelming "flood of information" that defined life in the late 1960s and early '70s.[3] He envisioned the tower as the habitat of *Homo movens*, the modern individual in an increasingly mobile society. Amid Japan's rapid economic growth and techno-industrial development, Kurokawa argued, the reach of the office had extended, taking over the home and the train commute. In response to Japan's emerging "information society" (*jōhōkashakai*), Kurokawa promoted the single-occupancy capsule as both a recuperative cocoon to shelter the individual from constant overstimulation and a quiet place do to some work after hours, if needed. He described it as "a place of rest to recover in modern society, an information base to develop ideas, and a home for urban dwellers who love the city center."[4] Kurokawa's sharp insight into these evolving societal dynamics, and his innovative response to them, made the Nakagin Capsule Tower a landmark of architectural foresight and a symbol of its era's profound social and technological transformations.

The Nakagin Capsule Tower is known as the most iconic realized example of Metabolism, an avant-garde Japanese movement that aimed to define a new philosophy and language for architecture following the devastation of World War II.

FIG. 2. Publicity photograph of a finished capsule interior, 1972

Formed in 1960, the Metabolist group brought together architects, critics, and designers, with Kurokawa as its youngest founding member.[5] In their manifesto-like first publication, the Metabolists boldly argued that architecture could catalyze Japan's evolution: "We believe design and technology should denote human vitality … we are trying to encourage the active metabolic development of our society through our proposals."[6] Of all the members, Kurokawa most fully embraced biological metaphors. He envisioned architecture capable of growth, adaptation, and transformation through what he called "metabolic cycles," whereby at predetermined intervals "only those parts that had lost their usefulness" would be replaced and, as a result, resources would be conserved.[7] For example, his 1961 Helix City Project for Tokyo, inspired by DNA's double helix, proposed an urban megastructure capable of dynamic expansion over time, both horizontally and vertically [FIG. 3]. Similarly, for the Nakagin Capsule Tower, Kurokawa envisioned an edifice that would undergo updates and changes over time. While the central cores could remain intact for sixty or so years, individual capsules could be replaced every twenty-five to thirty-five years—not to account for physical wear but to accommodate society's evolving needs.

While the Metabolists mostly explored their radical ideas on paper in the early 1960s, the Japan World Exposition in Osaka in 1970 offered them a major opportunity to bring their concepts to life for a wider audience. Kurokawa realized three structures: The most publicized was the "Beautilion" pavilion, a three-dimensional pipe-frame grid composed of two hundred prefabricated cross modules into which thirty stainless steel boxes were inserted; the structure housed exhibits for the Takara furniture company conglomerate [FIG. 4]. Less famous yet more consequential for Kurokawa's later studies on housing was the Capsule House—a full-scale prototype of a modular dwelling suspended from the space frame (also known as the "Big Roof") of the Theme Pavilion, whose design was overseen by his former teacher Kenzo Tange [FIG. 5]. Suspended almost 100 feet (30 meters) above the ground, the red-and-orange structure demonstrated Kurokawa's vision of "capsule architecture"—a new paradigm for building whereby prefabricated living units could be assembled into larger structures and modified over time [FIG. 6]. Giving preference to the individual over the nuclear family, the Capsule House consisted of three interconnected modules—for a man, a woman, and a child, each with a kidney-shaped bathroom—clustered around a circular corridor with a central tower of constantly playing televisions [FIG. 7]. In the context of Japan's hyperdense modernization after World War II, Kurokawa's design was more than just a demonstration of mass production in architecture. It was a call to carve out private space for *jiga*, a word that can be translated as "self." As Kurokawa emphatically argued, the capsule was thus not merely an architectural device but "a declaration of war in support of the restoration of [*jiga*], which has been lost in the process of modernization."[8]

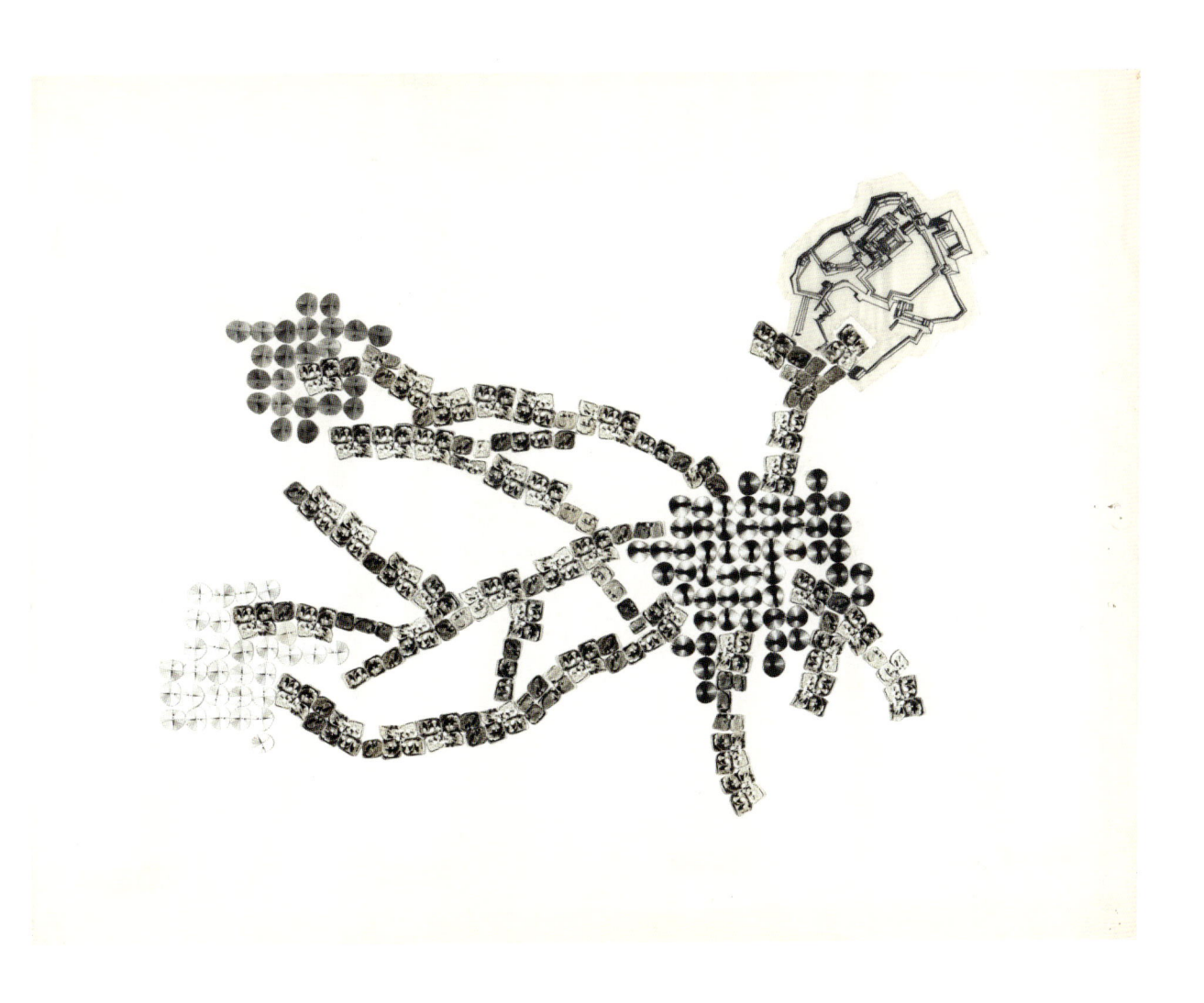

FIG. 3. Kisho Kurokawa (Japanese, 1934–2007). Plan for Helix City Project, Tokyo. 1961. Cut-and-pasted gelatin silver photographs and ink on cut-and-pasted tracing paper on paper, 21 ½ × 17 ½" (54.6 × 44.5 cm).
THE MUSEUM OF MODERN ART, NEW YORK. GIFT OF THE ARCHITECT

FIG. 4. Kisho Kurokawa Architect & Associates (Japan, est. 1962). Takara "Beautilion" pavilion, Expo '70, Osaka. 1968–70. Exterior view

FIG. 5. Kenzo Tange (Japanese, 1913–2005), with Koji Kamiya (Japanese, 1928–2014) and Asao Fukuda (Japanese). Space frame ("Big Roof") of the Theme Pavilion, Expo '70, Osaka. 1966–69. Photographed 1970

FIG. 6. Kisho Kurokawa Architect & Associates (Japan, est. 1962). Capsule House in the space frame of the Theme Pavilion, Expo '70, Osaka. 1969–70. View from below. 1970. Photograph: Tomio Ohashi

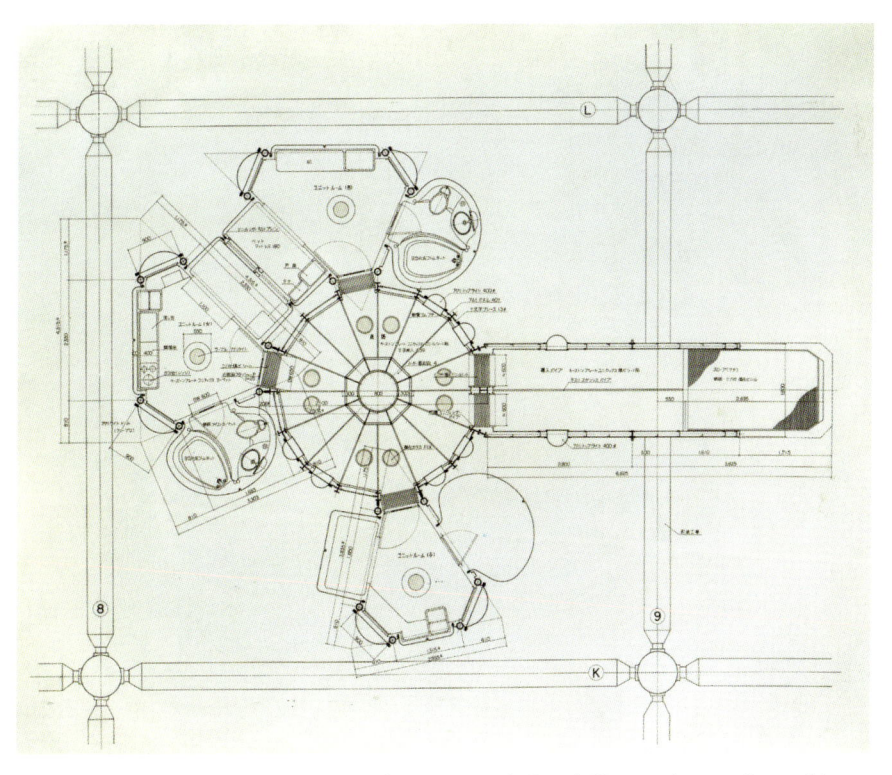

FIG. 7. Kisho Kurokawa Architect & Associates (Japan, est. 1962). Capsule House in the space frame of the Theme Pavilion, Expo '70, Osaka. 1970. Plan. Ink on polyester film, 29 ½ × 34 ⅝″ (75 × 88 cm). CENTRE POMPIDOU, MUSÉE NATIONAL D'ART MODERNE–CENTRE DE CRÉATION INDUSTRIELLE, PARIS. GIFT OF THE ARCHITECT

FIG. 8. Five types of capsules ("habitation," "transportation," "symbolic," "tool or device," and "living body"), in Kishō Kurokawa, "Oh! Saibogu no okite," *Space Design*, March 1969

FIG. 9. Women's palanquin. Japanese, Edo period, 1664. Lacquered wood with *maki-e*, 50 ⅛ × 35 ¾ × 48 ⅛″ (127.3 × 90.9 × 121.2 cm). TOKYO NATIONAL MUSEUM

Kurokawa wasn't the first among the Metabolists—or even globally—to propose the capsule as a spatial unit for the modern age. But he was the one savvy enough to develop and popularize a comprehensive theory around it. In "Oh! Saibogu no okite" (Oh! The code of the cyborg), an article for the magazine *Space Design* in 1969, he outlined eight polemical points for his conception of capsule architecture, which blurred the boundaries between biology and technology. "Just as a human with an artificial organ creates a new order that is neither human nor machine," he wrote, "the capsule transcends human and device."[9] His illustrations provided many examples of already existing capsule-like structures. These included transportation vehicles (from Airstream trailers to NASA's Project Mercury space capsule), mediators of biological and social processes (from live interpretation systems to window air-conditioning units), and even enclosures for the body between birth and death (from the amniotic sac to funerary boxes and coffins), among other provocative examples [**FIG. 8**]. He later expanded the main points of this article into his now famous "Capsule Declaration," which was further illustrated by historical Japanese designs of human-carried transit vehicles, such as the Edo-period *norimono* (palanquin) and the humbler Meiji-period *kago* (litter), made from bamboo and fabric [**FIG. 9**]. In weaving past and present examples into his vision of capsule architecture,

Kurokawa bridged traditional Japanese culture and modern technological society, making his theory influential well beyond the Metabolist movement.

Capitalizing on the publicity from Expo '70, Kurokawa reiterated his thesis on capsule architecture in *Kurokawa Kishō no sakuhin* (Kisho Kurokawa's work), which was published in the spring of 1970. Organized more like a visually striking magazine than a mundane architecture book, the highly graphic publication included a foldout poster featuring the original eight points of the "Capsule Declaration" [FIG. 10] and a seven-inch vinyl record of Kurokawa's voice, recreated by a computer out of previous recordings, reciting the text. Kurokawa's engaging way of communicating complex ideas about architecture's future eventually helped secure the commission for the Nakagin Capsule Tower. After Torizo Watanabe, the chairman of the Nakagin real estate company, saw the Takara "Beautilion" at Expo '70 and the widespread media attention surrounding Kurokawa's capsule architecture, he approached the architect to design a *manshon*—a branding term invented by Japanese real estate firms around the 1950s to refer to high-end apartment buildings—in Ginza. Initially, the plan included three capsule types—office, hotel, and residence—but the small interior size led Nakagin to focus solely on the typology of the business capsule. Although it was Kurokawa who secured the commission, the tower's realization was ultimately the result of a skilled team that worked together to bring the unprecedented building to life: The architect Nobuo Abe, who had overseen the Capsule House for Expo '70, led the design and handled the construction of the capsules; Aiko Mogi, the team's only female member, oversaw the building's elevations and all the drawings for the eight capsule layouts; Koji Shimosawa worked on the tower cores; and Kenjiro Ueda designed the shared plinth and oversaw the entire project. In addition to Kurokawa's office team, Gengo Matsui of O.R.S. Office, a professor of engineering at Waseda University, oversaw the structural study of the capsules, ensuring that their weight could be minimized.

With an extremely compressed timeline imposed by the Nakagin company, Kurokawa and his team worked tirelessly to finalize the building's design between August and December 1970. The iconic circular windows, for instance—which gave residents such as Takashi Fujino the feeling of inhabiting a camera body and looking out at the world through the lens—only appeared in Mogi's drawings on February 2, 1971, just a month before construction was set to begin [FIG. 11].[10] An early axonometric sketch by Abe highlights one of his key ideas for the capsule design: To maximize storage and space, all furniture should be built into the periphery of the interior [FIG. 12]. A passionate sailor from a young age, Abe modeled the capsule's compact interior after the restricted yet efficient interior of a sailing cabin, whose enveloping feeling he later described as "more like a kimono than a vehicle."[11] Although the Nakagin Capsule Tower remained physically anchored in Tokyo, its nautical cabin-like living units evoked the comfort

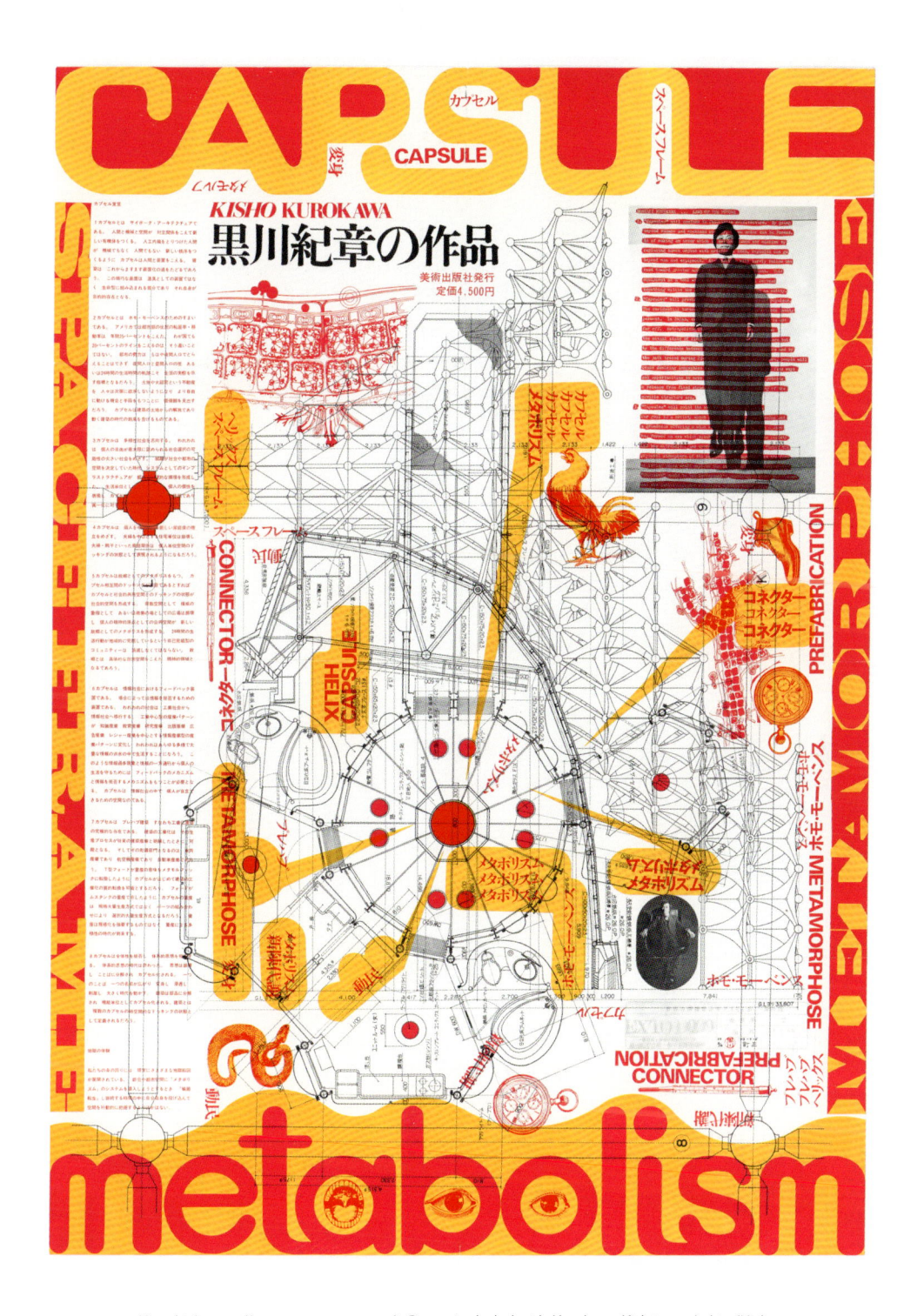

FIG. 10. Kiyoshi Awazu (Japanese, 1929–2009). Poster included with *Kurokawa Kishō no sakuhin* (Kisho Kurokawa's work) (Tokyo: Bijutsu Shuppan-sha, 1970). 1970. Screenprint, 40 3/16 × 28 9/16″ (102 × 72.5 cm).
THE MUSEUM OF MODERN ART ARCHIVES, LIBRARY, AND RESEARCH COLLECTIONS, NEW YORK

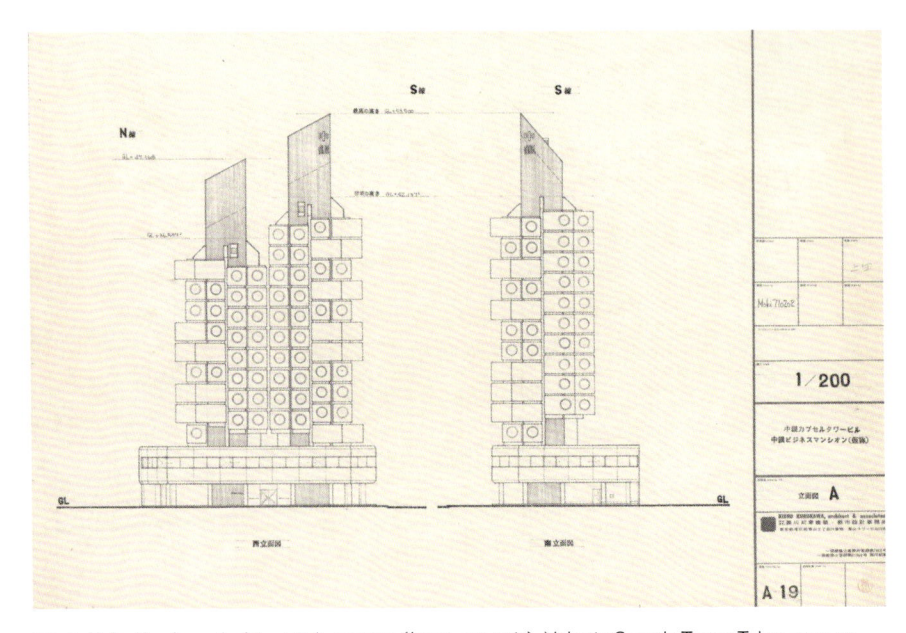

FIG. 11. Kisho Kurokawa Architect & Associates (Japan, est. 1962). Nakagin Capsule Tower, Tokyo. 1970–72. Elevations. Scale 1:200. February 2, 1971. Pencil on tracing paper, 16 ½ × 23 ⅛" (41.9 × 58.6cm). KISHO KUROKAWA ARCHITECT & ASSOCIATES, TOKYO

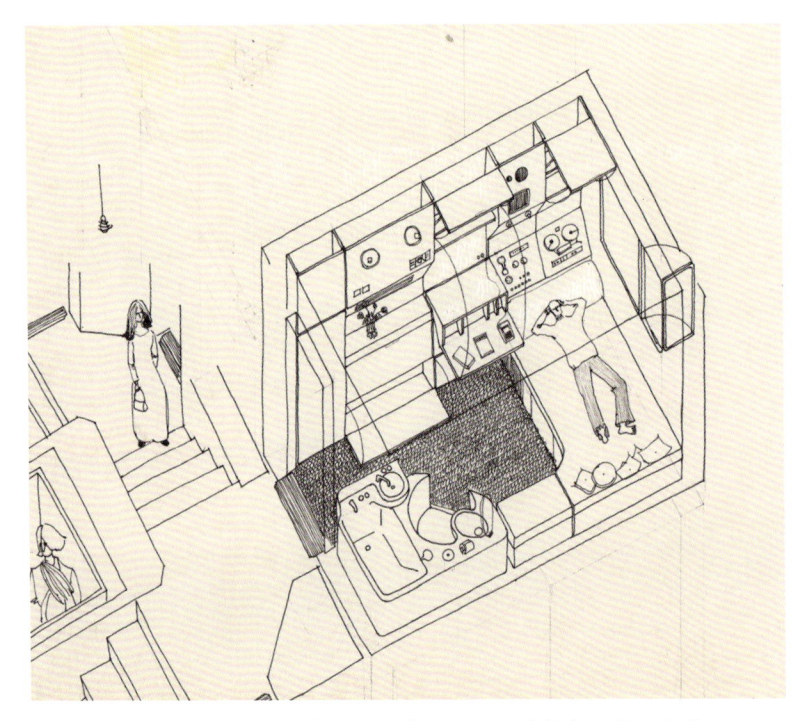

FIG. 12. Kisho Kurokawa Architect & Associates (Japan, est. 1962). Nakagin Capsule Tower, Tokyo. 1970–72. Cutaway axonometric sketch (detail). Scale 1:20. January 21, 1971. Marker on tracing paper, 16 ½ × 23 ⅛" (41.9 × 58.8 cm). KISHO KUROKAWA ARCHITECT & ASSOCIATES, TOKYO

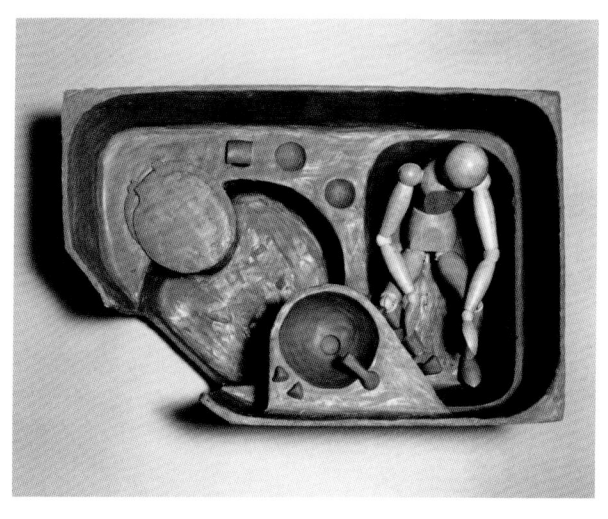

FIG. 13. Kisho Kurokawa Architect & Associates (Japan, est. 1962). Nakagin Tower Capsule. 1970–72. Model for testing the ergonomics of the foldout desk. C. 1970–71. KISHO KUROKAWA ARCHITECT & ASSOCIATES, TOKYO

FIG. 14. Kisho Kurokawa Architect & Associates (Japan, est. 1962). Nakagin Tower Capsule. 1970–72. Model for testing the ergonomics of the bathroom unit. C. 1970–71. KISHO KUROKAWA ARCHITECT & ASSOCIATES, TOKYO

of clothing, a natural extension of the body, and in this surrounding, a mental journey could be planned from the capsule's chart table–style desk.

Despite tight time constraints, Kurokawa's team crafted a series of study models that became crucial for addressing issues of scale, from how the building fit into its irregular Ginza site to how each capsule could maximize views of Tokyo. These models, especially interior ones, were vital for examining the ergonomics of the compact spaces. Archival photos reveal the team's hands-on, experimental approach: They positioned a wooden mannequin to assess whether cabinetry was accessible and built-in furniture could serve multiple functions. In one image, the mannequin sits on a foam-core bed, leaning toward the desk [**FIG. 13**]. Another, a top-down view of a detailed prefabricated bathroom model made of pliable plasticine to simulate the curves of the fiber-reinforced plastic (FRP) shell, shows the mannequin in the act of reaching for the sink from the bathtub [**FIG. 14**]. To confirm dimensioning, Mogi recalled, she "[glued] together pieces of paper to draw a full-scale plan of the capsule."[12] Based on the insights gained and Kurokawa's input, she then created the final construction drawings, densely annotated with the precise dimensions of every single component.

By early spring 1971, with a finalized design in place, Nakagin launched an inventive campaign to market the building. To introduce the novel concept of the "capsule *manshon*" to potential buyers, the company released *Business*

Capsule, a multipage brochure whose cover featured a vibrant color rendering of the building [**FIG. 15**]. Targeting the *Homo movens*, the campaign mirrored the tone and visual style of car catalogs. As with an automobile, the standard capsule frame could be customized with additional features for an extra cost. Kurokawa, an avid car enthusiast and owner of a Porsche 911S and a Lincoln Continental, explained in the brochure's introduction that "just as there is a full range of automobiles, from sedans to coupes to sports cars, a capsule house can serve numerous purposes—mini-office, studio, hotel, home, conference room, or urban villa—based on the equipment selected." Buyers could personalize their capsules with options ranging from standard to superdeluxe. Beyond basic amenities such as a 13-inch Sony color TV, an alarm clock, and a Sanyo refrigerator, custom-ordered features included a telephone handset, a pivoting desk lamp, stereo speakers, a Sony radio receiver and reel-to-reel tape recorder, and a state-of-the-art Sharp electronic calculator. While white was standard, buyers could choose from alternate color schemes in orange, blue, or black. To complete the pitch, Abe enlisted an illustrator from the Japanese magazine *Car Graphic*, who spent days at Kurokawa's office making the energetic drawings and sketches that illustrated the brochure, infusing the idea of purchasing a capsule with the thrill and freedom associated with a sleek roadster.

Nakagin's enticing portrayal of the building as an urban hideaway for commuting office workers went a step further with a trifold pamphlet featuring staged photos taken inside the pilot capsule (also known as "Capsule No. 1").[13] The cover photo portrayed a Japanese businessman, dressed in shirt and tie, smoking in bed while casually talking on the phone [**FIG. 16**]. Surrounded by a red Olivetti typewriter, Pioneer headphones, *Life* and *Newsweek* magazines, and a pack of Marlboro cigarettes, he was meant to embody a cosmopolitan urbanite whose interconnected capsule, Kurokawa argued, served as the "feedback device in the information society."[14] As the pamphlet further explained, each capsule's "information processing" equipment was complemented by the services of a "capsule lady," stationed in the lobby from 9 a.m. to 5 p.m., with optional housekeeping services also available through the building's management. This gendered division of roles, not atypical of the early 1970s, is evident in other promotional images, such as one from the newspaper *Asahi Shimbun*, in which an unidentified woman wearing a short skirt is shown seated at the desk; she presents the nape of her neck to the camera while browsing through a magazine [**FIG. 17**]. As contemporary critics and scholars have pointed out, capsules offered thrilling freedom to businessmen not only by allowing them to stay overnight in Tokyo's entertainment districts; it was also implied that their wives and children remained behind in suburban bedroom communities.[15] The capsule's promise of liberation for white-collar working men came at the cost of reinforcing these traditional and increasingly scrutinized divisions.

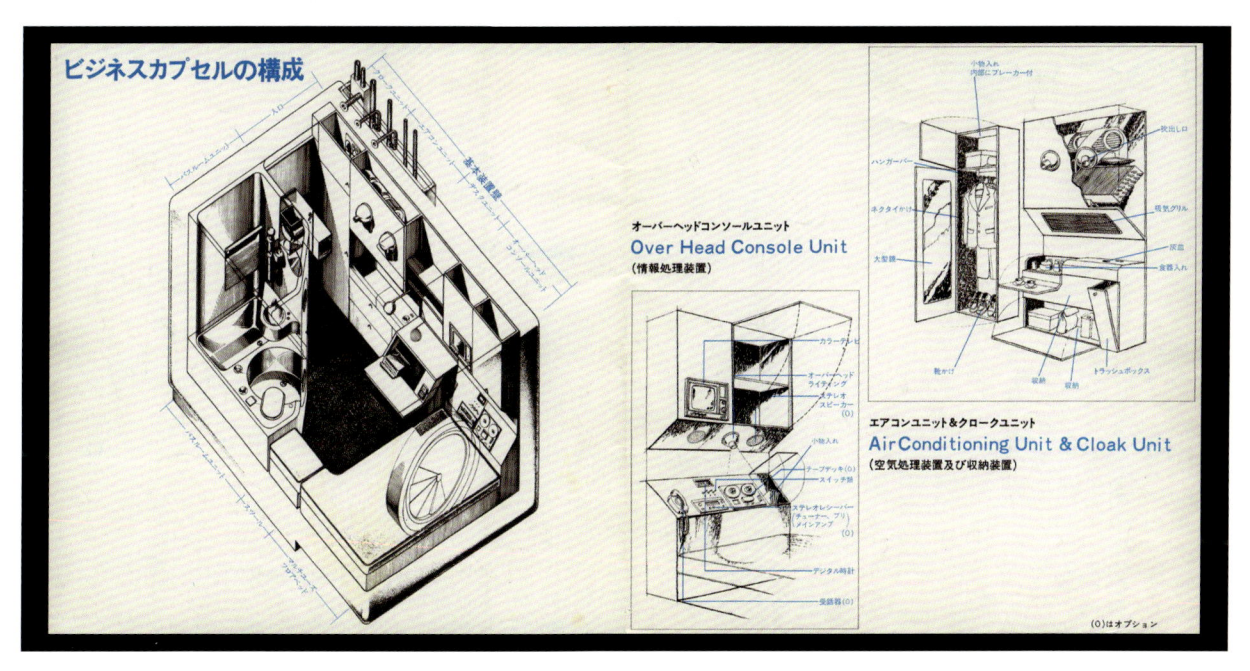

FIG. 15. Cover and spread from *Business Capsule*, a promotional brochure (in Japanese) for the Nagakin company, 1971

都心にマイペース空間をお持ちになりませんか

機能を徹底的に追求した21世紀住宅

中銀 カプセル マンシオン〈銀座〉

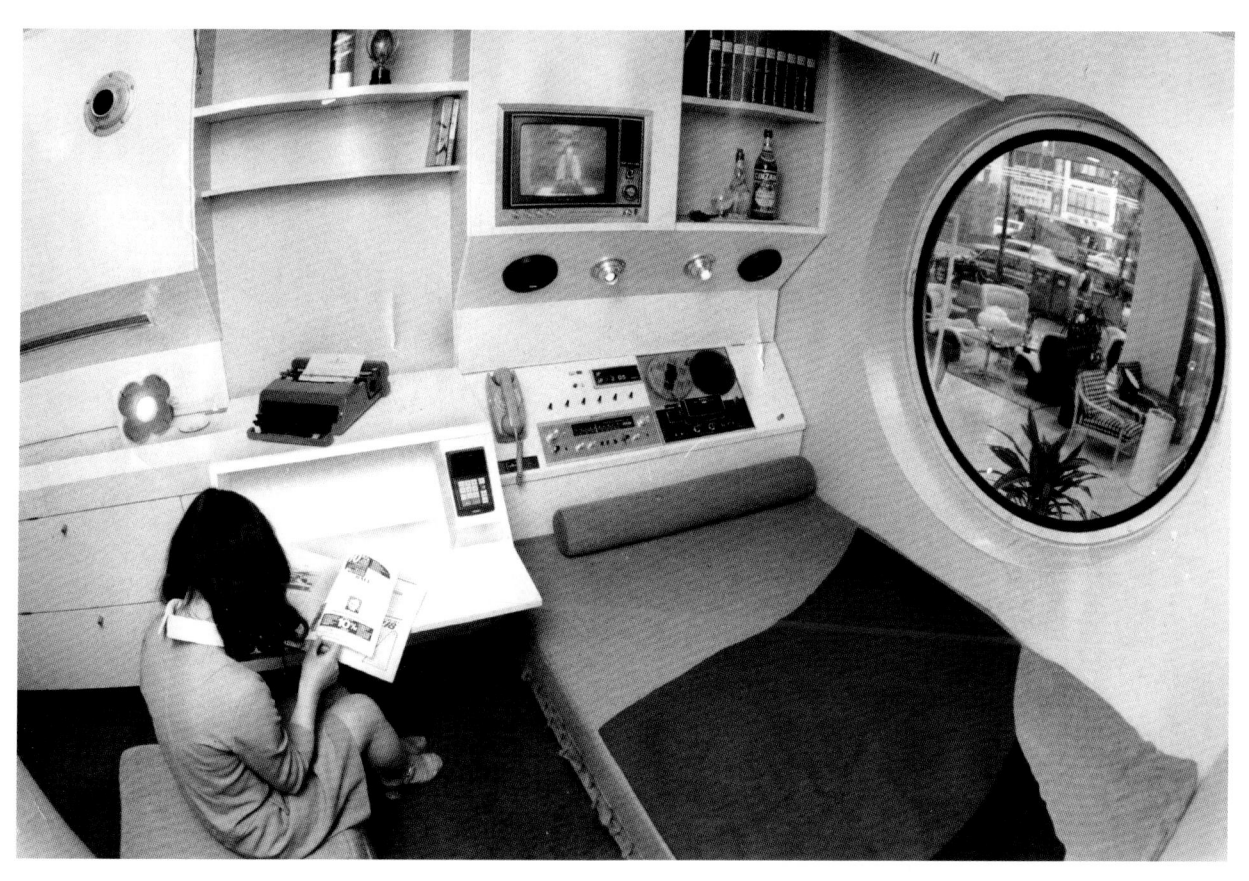

FIG. 17. Publicity image of a Nakagin pilot capsule, *Asahi Shimbun* newspaper, November 25, 1971

In addition to serving as the set for Nakagin's promotional photo shoot, the pilot capsule allowed Kurokawa's team the final finessing of the design. While the concrete plinth and towers were under construction in March 1970, the production of the 140 capsules began 450 miles away in Maibara, near Kyoto, at the Alna Koki plant, which Abe selected largely for its expertise in manufacturing shipping containers and locomotives. There, the lightweight-steel truss boxes that gave each capsule its structure were welded together and encased in the reinforced steel panels that formed its exterior surfaces [**FIG. 18**]. The Daimaru company, known for crafting space-efficient interiors for airplanes and ships, produced the handmade cabinetry and interior assembly. Once the building's vertical cores were completed, the first capsule—finished with a fresh coat of

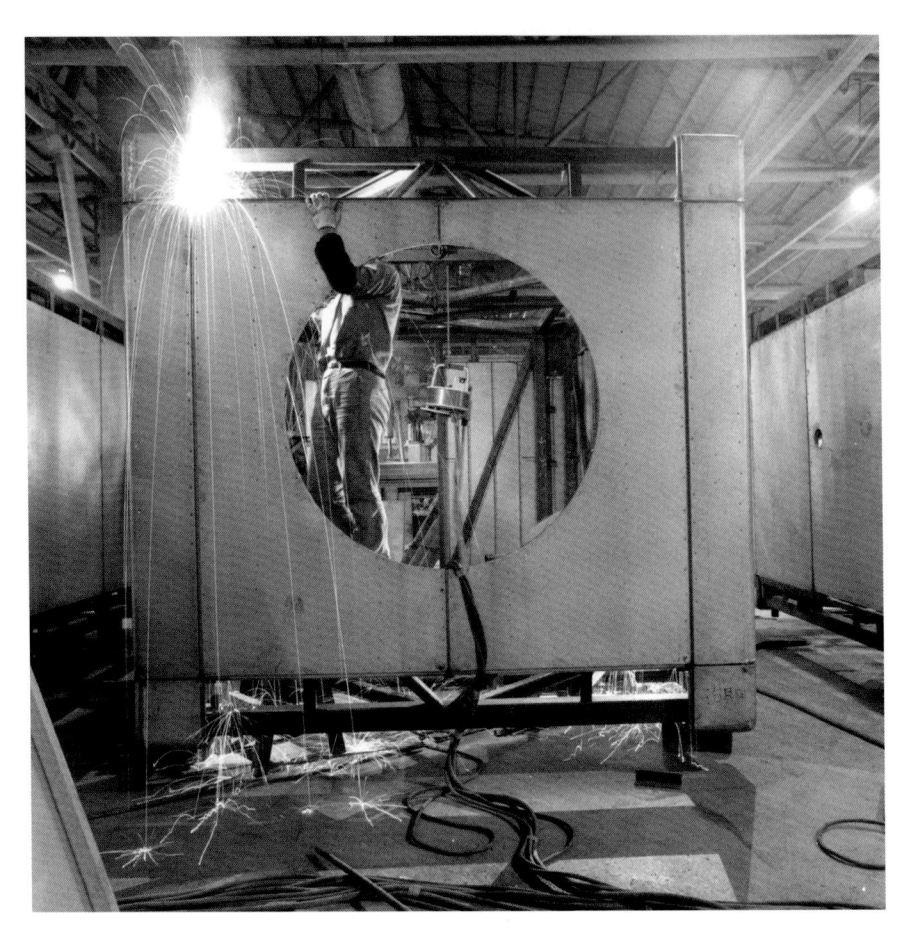

FIG. 18. Worker welding the skeleton of a prefabricated capsule, Alna Koki plant, Maibara, Shiga Prefecture, Japan, April–December, 1971. Photograph: Tomio Ohashi

vibrant white paint—arrived at the site in Ginza just before dawn on November 8, 1971. Over the next month and a half, trucks transported batches of capsules from Maibara to Tokyo each night for installation the following day. Workers of the Taisei construction company carefully hoisted each capsule by crane and maneuvered it into place in a precise aerial choreography, before attaching it to the building's vertical plumbing stacks **[FIG. 19]**. To personally witness and document the placement of the last capsule, Kurokawa arrived on-site equipped with his own camera early in the morning on December 24, 1971. Champagne was poured over the capsule's circular window, and colorful streamers fluttered as the capsule ascended, marking the rare transformation from an experimental architectural vision into tangible reality.

OPPOSITE: FIG. 19. Cranes hoisting a capsule to be attached to one of the two steel-and-concrete towers, November–December 1971. Photograph: Tomio Ohashi

Beyond its technical realization of an unprecedented design, the Nakagin Capsule Tower exemplifies how architecture can transcend its physical presence to become a cultural icon. Even before its official opening on April 5, 1972, the photogenic building had been showcased to a wide audience through both television and cinema. One of the building's capsules, freshly delivered in Tokyo and awaiting installation, was featured in a television segment by NHK, Japan's national broadcasting corporation. Just weeks later, the film *Godzilla vs. Gigan* was released in theaters, with a scene showing the destruction of a cruciform tower made of capsules featuring circular windows—an obvious reference to the Nakagin Capsule Tower—during a battle between Godzilla and alien monsters. Fittingly, following the building's completion, Taisei produced its own mini-film (*Capsule Manshon*, 1972) touting its ability to construct such an innovative design. The twenty-five-minute color documentary opens with Kurokawa's chronicle of the building's path from idea to physical structure. It closes with a fictionalized sequence doubling as an advertisement: a businessman arrives at the tower after a busy day, checks his mail in the reception area, takes the elevator to his capsule, and unwinds with a shower, a book, and music, while a view of the illuminated nocturnal city shimmers in the background [FIG. 20]. From nonfictional accounts to fully narrativized portrayals, these three examples of media coverage show how the image of the Nakagin Capsule Tower, rather than the building itself, became a powerful and alluring visual trope in popular culture.

The Nakagin Capsule Tower was a bold and unconventional addition to Tokyo's skyline. Its striking silhouette, characterized by the chamfered tower bulkheads, quickly became a point of urban curiosity for both locals and visitors, and a regular stop on a tourist bus route. In a frequently published photograph taken between late 1971 and early 1972 by the photographer Tomio Ohashi, Kurokawa's frequent collaborator, the building's unmistakable shape dominates the end of a busy traffic artery, visually representing the architecture of *Homo movens*—humanity in constant, rapid motion [FIG. 21]. While Ohashi's dynamic urban view centered the Nakagin Capsule Tower in the heart of Tokyo's fast-paced life, an unpublished photograph taken by a member of Kurokawa's office offers a starkly different perspective [FIG. 22]. Captured from a side street, the image reveals a slower-paced reality: Ginza's low wooden structures are still in view, people walk along the right side of the street, and hand-pulled rickshaws (*jinrikisha*) are parked in a row on the left, suggesting a more traditional, unhurried way of life. In the distance, the Nakagin Capsule Tower rises like a futuristic anomaly. The building thus not only came to symbolize Kurokawa's radical architectural proposition but also became emblematic of the profound transformations Tokyo, and especially Ginza, would undergo over the following decades.

In its first year of operation, the Nakagin Capsule Tower achieved the rare combination of both critical and commercial success. For Kurokawa's office,

FIG. 20. Stills from the promotional film *Capsule Manshon* (1972) showing a nomadic businessman arriving at his capsule and spending the evening there

FIG. 21. View of the Nakagin Capsule Tower nearing completion, taken from one of Tokyo's main traffic arteries, 1971–72. Photograph: Tomio Ohashi

FIG. 22. View of the Nakagin Capsule Tower from Kobikicho Street in Ginza, Tokyo, 1971–72

it generated significant attention in the architectural press, with journals from Japan, Europe, and the United States eager to profile the project.[16] Meanwhile, the Nakagin company reported thousands of inquiries from prospective buyers, despite the capsule's price of three million yen—fifty percent more than the cost of a typical apartment. Enthused by the demand, Watanabe soon relocated Nakagin's headquarters to the building's plinth, aligning the company's identity with the image of the tower [FIG. 23]. Responding to market interest, especially from small and medium-sized enterprises in rural areas, Nakagin enlisted Kurokawa's services again, this time to assess the feasibility of additional towers throughout the city. In keeping with Metabolist principles, Kurokawa's team explored replicating the structure and linking multiple towers to create urban megastructures. To showcase their proposition, a preexisting wooden model of the building [FIG. 24] was hurriedly integrated into a larger presentation model that included a speculative twin complex across the street [FIG. 25]. More poignantly, an extension of the original plinth created a raised walkway that connected the two towers with a smaller capsule structure, which in fact was a replica of Kurokawa's own vacation home, Capsule House K, completed in 1973. For a brief moment it seemed like Kurokawa was one step closer to realizing not just an additional new building but his broader Metabolist vision of interconnected infrastructure for Tokyo.

FIG. 23. Nakagin company headquarters after relocation to the tower's plinth, c. 1972. Photograph: Tomio Ohashi

FIG. 24. Kisho Kurokawa Architect & Associates (Japan, est. 1962). Nakagin Capsule Tower, Tokyo. 1970–72. Photograph of a wood presentation model. C. 1971–72. KISHO KUROKAWA ARCHITECT & ASSOCIATES, TOKYO

FIG. 25. Kisho Kurokawa Architect & Associates (Japan, est. 1962). Nakagin Capsule Tower, Tokyo. 1970–72. Photograph of an enlarged wood-and-brass model showcasing expansion possibilities. c. 1972. KISHO KUROKAWA ARCHITECT & ASSOCIATES, TOKYO

The euphoria was short-lived, however. The international oil crisis of 1973, which began toward the end of the year, abruptly halted any plans for additional iterations of the tower. A survey by Nakagin revealed that in just a few months, construction costs had skyrocketed. More critically, concerns over Japan's dependence on imported oil shifted consumer priorities. As fuel prices soared, the appeal of owning a compact second apartment in the city faded, with many buyers opting for larger, more comfortable primary residences outside the city. These obstacles, along with a shortage of suitable land in Tokyo, resulted in the indefinite shelving of the expansion plans. Nevertheless, the original Nakagin Capsule Tower continued to thrive. For its first fifteen years, the building maintained full occupancy, and as Ginza rapidly developed during the 1980s "bubble economy," the market value of the capsules tripled. In line with Nakagin's ambitions, the quirky edifice became an increasingly sought-after address and real estate investment. The fact that Kurokawa himself, by then a public figure, retained a unit for use by his office staff—the "legendary" capsule A1302, one among only a handful ordered in the black color scheme (a playful nod to his name, as *kuro* means "black" in Japanese)—further enhanced the building's attractiveness and mystique.[17]

Despite its initial thriving, the survival of the Nakagin Capsule Tower became an uphill battle over time. As Kurokawa had stated shortly after the project's completion in 1972, the building was expected to have a sixty-year life-span, with the capsules needing replacement at about the halfway point because of shifting societal needs. By the late 1980s, however, as taller buildings sprang up and a construction boom for new residential properties took hold, the structure had already begun to lose its novelty. In the early 1990s, Japan's bubble economy collapsed, causing a housing surplus and plummeting property values. As residents moved out of the building, funds for maintenance dwindled, and rainwater pooling on the flat tops of the capsules began to cause corrosion. By the mid-1990s, the colorful stairways—once vividly painted in "coral" red and orange, and "peacock" blue and turquoise, as a promotional pamphlet had specified—were covered with somber grays. With the capsules nearing their intended "expiry date," Kurokawa hoped the building would undergo its metabolic cycle. Beginning in 1998, his office proposed plans to renew the capsules—either refurbishing and reinstalling them or replacing them entirely, as a way to literally imbue the building with new life. But any scenario involving refurbishment would have required the prohibitively expensive removal of asbestos insulation, which had been banned in Japan in 1975. Despite Kurokawa's personal efforts and pleas, an affordable solution remained out of reach. Even though the design was premised on the easy replacement of capsules, the narrow spacing between them meant that in practice, all the units above a particular capsule had to be removed before it could be detached. Meanwhile, the capsules' individual ownership further impeded a decision

FIG. 26. Noritaka Minami (American, born Japan 1981). *A905 I*, from the series 1972 (2010–22). 2018. Archival pigment print, 40 × 50″ (101.6 × 127 cm)

about what should be done—some owners prioritized preservation, while others were swayed by the financial lure of the site's redevelopment.

Kurokawa's death in the fall of 2007, only a few months after the building's management association approved a plan to sell and redevelop, further dampened any ongoing efforts to secure a feasible plan for its preservation. The year before, the Japan chapter of the architecture-preservation organization Docomomo listed the tower among its 125 most significant examples of modern architecture in the country, but when the developer that eventually agreed to purchase the building filed for bankruptcy, the structure's fate was thrown into limbo once again. By the early 2010s, parts of it were already beyond repair. Many capsules, long past their replacement date, suffered extensive leaks, making them unsuitable to inhabit.

Despite its deteriorating condition, the Nakagin Capsule Tower never ceased to possess an almost inexplicable charm. To the architect Takashi Fujino, who lived in the building from 2000 to 2006, living in capsule B803 often felt like "driving a cranky classic car," full of character yet constantly in need of care.[18] When the photographer Noritaka Minami began documenting the tower in 2010, he found it veiled in netting to protect pedestrians from falling debris, with some of its units, especially those whose tenants had not returned in a long time, severely damaged **[FIG. 26]**. By 2012, the central air-conditioning stopped working permanently, leading to overheating during the summer and further damage due to condensation. Yet, notwithstanding the building's sad state of decay, Minami was captivated by how the majority of capsules remained lively and personalized. Unlike the spartan, staged publicity images from 1972, he noticed, the capsules had "accumulated the passage of time and the traces of people who had inhabited them."[19] In fact, immediately upon the building's completion, residents had started "metabolizing" the interior of their individual capsules, removing the built-in cabinetry for more space or new furniture, resurfacing floors and repainting walls, installing air-conditioning units, and opening additional windows to let in more light. The building, aging yet adaptive, continued to inspire its residents to care for it.

Unexpectedly, during its final decade, from 2012 to 2022, the Nakagin Capsule Tower was once again a buzzing and lively place. Even in its declining condition, which put almost half of the capsules permanently out of use, there was once again a long waiting list of prospective tenants eager to move in. The unusually low rents for the prime location attracted a diverse group of creative individuals—architects, designers, photographers, editors, writers, filmmakers, and musicians, among others. Many of them not only were deeply aware of the building's historical significance but also became actively involved in demanding its preservation. Among them was Takayuki Sekine, a retired manager, who learned about the building from an architecture guidebook and with his wife, Yumiko, subsequently purchased capsule B1004 (featured on the cover of this publication). He specifically sought a unit that retained its original design features and even searched auctions for memorabilia, such as a lamp shaped like the building, which Nakagin had given to the original capsule owners in 1972 [FIG. 27].

Takayuki Sekine would join the Nakagin Capsule Tower Preservation and Restoration Project, a small group of residents that assembled in 2014 under the slogan #SaveNakagin to raise awareness and secure financial backing to save the building. Even though Kurokawa envisioned the Nakagin Capsule Tower as a cluster of 140 individuals in separate units, its capsules became gathering spaces for the residents group to strategize and socialize. Tatsuyuki Maeda, a founding member, recalled that "some capsules would open every evening, like a pub, and hold social gatherings—up to fifteen people!" [FIG. 28][20] Furthermore, each resident continued the series of smaller "metabolic cycles" of the capsule interiors, adapting their unit to meet their own needs and desires. Over its first forty years, Nakagin's "business capsules" had been creatively repurposed into student rooms, tearooms, party spaces, storage units, galleries, and even "pink capsules" for intimate encounters; the final group of residents used them as primary living spaces or second homes, or turned them into libraries, film studios, writing retreats, architecture ateliers, live streaming studios, and DJ booths, to name but a few examples [FIG. 29]. Chie Nomura, who had planned to move

FIG. 27. Takayuki Sekine demonstrating the commemorative lamp given by the Nakagin company to the first 140 capsule owners in 1972

FIG. 28. A social gathering in one of the capsules, 2016

in for a month but ended up staying seven, recalled that her unit B703 would turn into a "capsule theater" with the help of a digital projector and blue lighting—a peaceful sanctuary for watching films while the city buzzed outside **[FIG. 30]**. Despite their size—a little less than "six tatami mats," as Kurokawa often explained—the capsules proved to contain an infinitely flexible space, offering comfort over confinement and fostering a deep sense of attachment. "The reason why everyone is addicted to capsules," Maeda noted, "is that they provide a small but cozy space."[21]

Although it was designed around the idea of allowing each resident to retreat to their own private bubble, the Nakagin Capsule Tower paradoxically acted as a social condenser. As its infrastructure systems failed, the relationships among its inhabitants strengthened. During earthquakes, elevator outages forced residents to spend more time together in the lobby. Water leaks also pushed them to gather temporarily, creating a sense of extended family. After the central water boiler failed, groups of residents would visit Konparu-yu, a historic public bathhouse (*sentō*) nearby in Ginza. The changing seasons also

FOLLOWING SPREAD: FIG. 29. Images from *Nakagin Capsule Style* (Tokyo: Soshisha, 2020) showing the capsules used (page 34, top to bottom) as a second home, an architecture tour showpiece, and a film-editing studio; and (page 35, top to bottom) a home base, a writing retreat, and a DJ booth

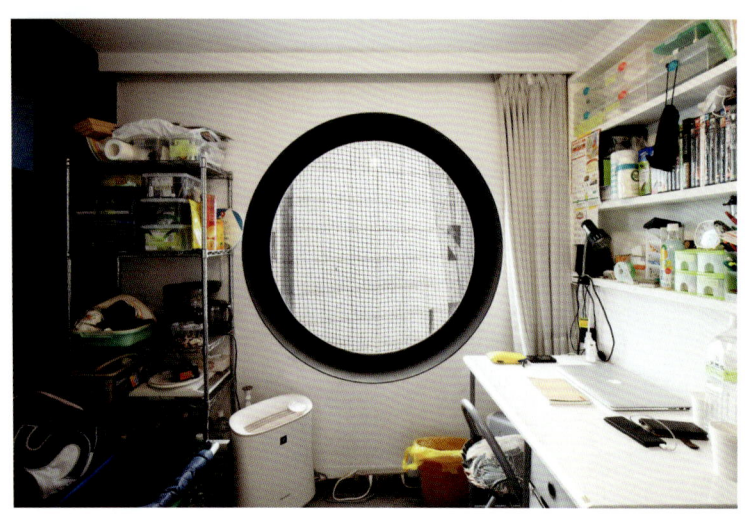

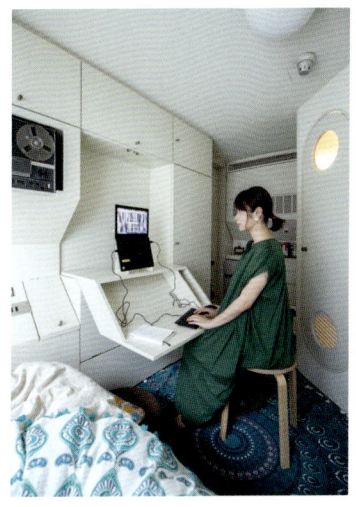

FIG. 30. Chie Nomura in her private "capsule theater," c. 2022

shaped how shared spaces were used. "Especially in summer," Maeda recalled, "the three egress bridges connecting the towers on the back side of the building were used as public space," with residents grilling fish, setting off fireworks, and gathering outside.[22] In winter, they came together for *mochitsuki*, the traditional rice-pounding process, in celebration of the new year. Oddly enough, the building developed a reputation as a lively, close-knit community. Despite its original branding as a hub of urban anonymity for male workers, in its final years, more than half the Nakagin Capsule Tower's occupants were women, marking its transformation into a vibrant and socially diverse space of cohabitation.

Despite years of negotiations between the Nakagin company, the association of capsule owners and residents, and potential external parties—investors, developers, and others—a financially viable solution to save the building proved elusive. Meanwhile, the prolonged lack of maintenance rendered the structure seismically unsafe. In 2021, the long-dreaded announcement confirming the building's impending teardown sparked strong reactions—both in Japan and, perhaps even

FIG. 31. ARCHI HATCH (Japan, est. 2018), Yuta Tokunaga (Japanese, born 1980). Nakagin Capsule Tower 3D Archive: The Last Scan. February 2, 2022. Photogrammetry model. View of the two towers and select capsules without facades

FIG. 32. ARCHI HATCH (Japan, est. 2018), Yuta Tokunaga (Japanese, born 1980). Nakagin Capsule Tower 3D Archive: The Last Scan. February 2, 2022. Photogrammetry model. View of the reception and mailboxes area

more intensely, from the international architectural community. In a thoughtful effort to preserve the memory of the building before it was dismantled, the residents group produced several photographic publications, conducted a series of video interviews with twenty of the last residents inside their capsules, and collaborated with Yuta Tokunaga, a specialist in 360-degree architectural documentation, to create a 3D archive of the entire structure using digital photogrammetry [**FIGS. 31, 32**]. The demolition began on April 12, 2022, and was completed by October 1 of the same year [**FIG. 33**]. The filmmaker Masa Yoshikawa, who had used capsule A408 as his editing studio, recounts that the residents group rented a small space across from the site so that they could witness and document "the last moments of the capsule tower."[23] Koe-chan, a cosplay DJ who instantly decided that she wanted to become a resident of the "Lego-like building" when she first saw it from the adjacent highway, remembers watching the removal of each capsule by crane, as they had first been installed [**FIG. 34**]: "There was something so beautiful about seeing the capsules fly up in the air again. I was so sad about the demolition process itself, but I wanted to be there to witness it."[24]

Fortunately, the Nakagin Capsule Tower has not entirely disappeared. The Nakagin Capsule Tower Preservation and Restoration Project led a logistically and financially complex campaign to preserve twenty-three of the building's capsules. The selected capsules were carefully removed from the building, safely stripped of their asbestos insulation, and divided into two groups based on their condition: nine were reduced to their steel armatures, while fourteen were meticulously restored to fully furnished units using the best salvaged parts from across the building. Thanks to the generosity of the project's team, The Museum of Modern Art was able to acquire one of the latter units: capsule A1305, which once occupied the tower's pinnacle. After crossing the Pacific Ocean and the breadth of the United States to reach its new home in New York, this capsule served as the centerpiece of *The Many Lives of the Nakagin Capsule Tower,* an exhibition showcasing the multivalent legacy of the iconic building, in the summer of 2025 [**FIGS. 35–37**]. Although a fragment can never fully embody the spirit of the entire architectural project in its original setting, the Nakagin Capsule Tower offers a rare instance in which its designers imagined that the self-contained units indeed might one day journey over oceans. As of this writing,

FIG. 33. Noritaka Minami (American, born Japan 1981). *Remnants,* from the series 1972 (2010–22). 2022. Archival pigment print, 40 × 50" (101.6 × 127 cm)

FIG. 34. A capsule from the Nakagin Capsule Tower in midair during the building's dismantling, 2022

the capsules have found new homes across Japan and far beyond—in Asia, Australia, the Middle East, Europe, and North America—embodying the legacy of an architectural dream that continues to travel the world.

While some may argue that the Nakagin Capsule Tower has been lost forever, one could also say it has simply entered a new "metabolic cycle"—just not the one Kurokawa originally envisioned. The twenty-three preserved capsules, along with the extensive accompanying documentation—drawings, photographs, videos, stories, interviews, social media posts, and 3D models—now constitute a living archive that marks a new phase in the building's existence. Often mistakenly labeled a failed utopian project, the Nakagin Capsule Tower, which occupied its site for more than half a century, was not only a remarkable manifestation of architectural thought but also a daily, lived experience for hundreds, if not thousands, of devoted residents. As a unique case study, it continues to provoke meaningful discussions on the future of urban density, sustainable housing, and the extension of architecture's life-span through replaceable components. Ultimately, the Nakagin Capsule Tower demonstrates that the true power of architecture lies not merely in its physical form but in its ability to advance conversations and foster human connections—to build vibrant communities even in impermanence.

NOTES

In writing this essay, the author drew information and details from the sources cited in the footnotes as well as the following:

Completion of the Nakagin Capsule Tower Building [brochure in Japanese] (Tokyo: Nakagin, 1972); Takashi Hashimoto, "Metabolism's New Voyage" [in Japanese], *Nikkei Architecture*, no. 8–25 (2022): 74–81; Jin Hidaka, "Nakagin Capsule Tower Building," circular, XXIV UIA Congress: Design 2050, Tokyo, 2011; Aki Ishida, "Encapsulated Masculine Dreams: The Cultural and Material Impermanence of the Nakagin Capsule Tower," *sITA: studii de Istoria şi Teoria Arhitecturii*, no. 10 (2022): 199–212; Kishō Kurokawa, *Kurokawa Kishō: mirai o sōzō suru kenchiku* [Kisho Kurokawa: architecture of metabolism] (Tokyo: Nobel Shobo, 1969); Thomas Leslie, "Just What Is It That Makes Capsule Homes So Different, So Appealing? Domesticity and the Technological Sublime, 1945 to 1975," *Space and Culture* 9, no. 2 (May 2006): 180–94; Peter Šenk, *Capsules: Typology of Other Architecture* (Milton Park, UK: Routledge, 2017); Tatsuyuki Maeda and Yuka Yoshida, "Heritage in Danger: The Real Reason Why Nakagin Capsule Tower Was Never Metabolized," *Docomomo Journal*, no. 65 (July 2021): 118–20; Noritaka Minami, *1972* (Heidelberg: Kehrer, 2015); Matthew Mullane, "Capsular Japan: The 'Information Society' and Kisho Kurokawa's Nakagin Capsule Tower" (master's thesis, School of the Art Institute of Chicago, 2012); Filipe Magalhães and Ana Luisa Soares, "Routine metabolista / The Metabolist Routine," *Domus*, no. 969 (May 2013): 76–83; Yuki Solomon, "Kurokawa's Capsule Tower to Be Razed," *Architectural Record* 195, no. 6 (June 2007): 34; Akiko Tanabe, "The Nakagin Capsule Tower Building as a 'Standard' for Measuring Urban Distortion" [in Japanese], *Nikkei Architecture*, no. 289 (April 20, 1987): 140–44; Toshihiko Suzuki, "Symposium," in *Kurokawa Kishō no kapuseru kenchiku / Capsule Architecture by Kisho Kurokawa*, trans. Yuki Sugihara (Tokyo: Opa, 2022), 160–65; and Shingo Wakabayashi, "The Takara Beautilion," *Japan Architect*, no. 164 (May–June 1970): 130–31.

The author is grateful for information provided by Hajime Yatsuka, architect and emeritus professor at Shibaura Institute of Technology, Tokyo, in an interview on May 28, 2024; as well as by former residents of the Nakagin Capsule Tower, including Tatsuyuki Maeda in an interview on May 23, 2024; Kenichi Muranaka, Wakana Nitta ("Koe-chan"), Chie Nomura, Shojiro Okuyama, and Masahiro Yoshikawa in an interview on May 27, 2024; and Takayuki Sekine and Yumiko Sekine in an interview on May 29, 2024.

The author would also like to thank Paula Vilaplana de Miguel, Joëlle Martin, Y. L. Lucy Wang, and Maeda for their assistance and support.

1. Kisho Kurokawa, *Metabolism in Architecture* (London: Studio Vista, 1977), 105.
2. See Arthur Drexler, *Transformations in Modern Architecture* (New York: The Museum of Modern Art, 1979), 132–33; Barry Bergdoll and Peter Christensen, *Home Delivery: Fabricating the Modern Dwelling* (New York: The Museum of Modern Art, 2008), 144–47; and Doryun Chong, *Tokyo, 1955–1970: A New Avant-Garde* (New York: The Museum of Modern Art, 2012), 31–32.
3. Kurokawa, "Oh! Saibogu no okite" [Oh! The code of the cyborg], *Space Design*, no. 52 (March 1969): 50; English translation as "Capsule Declaration," in Suzuki, *Capsule Architecture by Kisho Kurokawa*, n.p. Kurokawa later expanded his declaration in *Kurokawa Kishō: mirai o sōzō suru kenchiku*, 187–204; English translation in *Metabolism in Architecture*, 75–85.

4. Kurokawa, "The Era of Capsule Housing," in *Business Capsule* [brochure in Japanese] (Tokyo: Nakagin, n.d. [1971]), n.p. Translation by the author.

5. Along with Kurokawa, the founding members of the Metabolism group were the architects Kiyonori Kikutake, Masato Otaka, and Fumihiko Maki, as well as the critic Noboru Kawazoe, the industrial designer Kenji Ekuan, and the graphic designer Kiyoshi Awazu. On the complex genealogy and history of the movement, see Yatsuka, *Metaborizumu nekusasu* [Metabolism nexus] (Tokyo: Ohmsha, 2011); Yatsuka et al., *Metaborizumu no mirai toshi: sengo Nihon ima yomigaeru fukkō no yume to bijon / Metabolism, The City of the Future: Dreams and Visions of Reconstruction in Postwar and Present-Day Japan* (Tokyo: Mori Art Museum, 2011); Rem Koolhaas and Hans Ulrich Obrist, *Project Japan: Metabolism Talks*, ed. Kayoko Ota and James Westcott (Cologne: Taschen, 2011).

6. Kiyonori Kikutake et al., *Metaborizumu 1960: Toshi e no teian / Metabolism 1960: The Proposals for New Urbanism* (Tokyo: Bijutsu Shuppan-sha, 1960), n.p.

7. Kurokawa, *Metabolism in Architecture*, 32.

8. Kurokawa, *Metabolism in Architecture*, 36.

9. Kurokawa, "Capsule Declaration," in *Capsule Architecture by Kisho Kurokawa*, n.p.

10. Takashi Fujino, interview by the author, May 29, 2024.

11. Nobuo Abe, "Interview: Nakagin Capsule Tower Building Interior Designer Nobuo Abe Talks About the Behind-the Scenes Story of Capsule Production and His Encounter with Kisho Kurokawa" [in Japanese], by Nanae Yamazaki, *Yadokari*, July 11, 2015, yadokari.net/interview/28783/. Translation by the author.

12. Aiko Mogi, in Suzuki, "Symposium," 164. Translation amended by the author.

13. *A 21st-Century Home That Thoroughly Pursues Functionality: Nakagin Capsule Manshon (Ginza)* [brochure in Japanese] (Tokyo: Nakagin, n.d. [1971]).

14. Kurokawa, "Capsule Declaration," n.p.

15. Koolhaas and Obrist, *Project Japan*, 388; Ishida, "Encapsulated Masculine Dreams," 204–6, 212.

16. See, for example, "Capsule d'habitation. Noriaki Kurokawa, architecte," *L'Architecture d'aujourd'hui*, no. 161 (April–May 1972): 24; Kenjiro Ueda, "Nakagin Capsule Tower Building by Kisho N. Kurakawa Architect & Associates" [in Japanese], *Kenchiku bunka* 27, no. 308 (June 1972): 128–30; "Kurokawa—Wohnkapselsystem" [Kurokawa—residential capsule system], *Deutsche Bauzeitung* 106, no. 12 (1972): 1312; Paolo Riani, "Kurokawa and His Capsules," *Architectural Record* 153, no. 2 (February 1973): 109–14; "Le Capsule di Kurokawa: Nakagin Capsule Building, Ginza, Tokyo," *Domus*, no. 520 (March 1973): 3–6; and Yasuo Uesaka, "Kurokawa," *Architecture Plus* 2, no. 1 (January–February 1974): 96–124.

17. Minami, interview by the author and Joëlle Martin, February 7, 2024; Maeda, interview by the author.

18. Fujino, "The Future Is Not Over: Five Years and Five Months at the Nakagin Capsule Tower and Afterward" [in Japanese], *Shinkenchiku Online*, December 28, 2022. Translation by the author.

19. Minami, interview by the author.

20. Maeda, interview by the author.

21. Maeda, "Story after Demolition of Nakagin Capsule Tower Building: An Interview with Tatsuyuki Maeda," by Suzuki, in *Capsule Architecture by Kisho Kurokawa*, 222–23.

22. Maeda, interview by the author.

23. Yoshikawa, interview by the author.

24. Koe-chan, interview by the author.

43

FOR FURTHER READING

Bergdoll, Barry, and Peter Christensen. *Home Delivery: Fabricating the Modern Dwelling*. New York: The Museum of Modern Art, 2008.

Guiheux, Alain. *Kisho Kurokawa, architecte: Le Métabolisme, 1960–1975*. Paris: Éditions du Centre Georges Pompidou, 1997.

Ishida, Aki. "Encapsulated Masculine Dreams: The Cultural and Material Impermanence of the Nakagin Capsule Tower." *sITA: studii de Istoria şi Teoria Arhitecturii*, no. 10 (2022): 199–212.

Koolhaas, Rem, and Hans Ulrich Obrist. *Project Japan: Metabolism Talks*. Edited by Kayoko Ota and James Westcott. Cologne: Taschen, 2011.

Kurokawa, Kisho. *Homo mōbensu* [Homo movens]. Tokyo: Chūō Kōronsha, 1969.

———. *Metabolism in Architecture*. London: Studio Vista, 1977.

Lin, Zhongjie. "Nakagin Capsule Tower: Revisiting the Future of the Recent Past." *Journal of Architectural Education* 65, no. 1 (October 2011): 13–32.

Nakagin Capsule Tower Building Preservation and Restoration Project. *Nakagin Kapuseru Tawā biru: saigo no kiroku / Nakagin Capsule Tower: The Last Record*. Tokyo: Soshisha, 2022.

Riani, Paolo. "Kurokawa and His Capsules." *Architectural Record* 153, no. 2 (February 1973): 109–14.

Suzuki, Toshihiko. *Kurokawa Kishō no kapuseru kenchiku / Capsule Architecture by Kisho Kurokawa*. Tokyo: Opa, 2022.

Yatsuka, Hajime, et al. *Metaborizumu no mirai toshi: sengo Nihon ima yomigaeru fukkō no yume to bijon / Metabolism, The City of the Future: Dreams and Visions of Reconstruction in Postwar and Present-Day Japan*. Tokyo: Mori Art Museum, 2011.

Leadership support for this publication is provided by the Kate W. Cassidy Foundation.

Produced by the Department of Publications
The Museum of Modern Art, New York

Leadership support for this publication is provided by
the Kate W. Cassidy Foundation.

Michelle Kuo, Chief Curator at Large and Publisher
Curtis R. Scott, Associate Publisher
Hannah Kim, Business and Marketing Director
Joseph Mohan, Production Director

Edited by Elizabeth Tucker
Series designed by Miko McGinty and Rita Jules
Layout by Amanda Washburn
Production by Matthew Pimm
Editorial project management by Emily Hall
Proofread by Jackie Neudorf
Printed and bound by Offset Yapımevi, Istanbul

This book is typeset in Ideal Sans.
The paper is 150 gsm Magno Satin.

Published by The Museum of Modern Art
11 West 53 Street
New York, NY 10019-5497
www.moma.org

ISBN: 978-1-63345-173-5

Distributed in the United States and Canada by
ARTBOOK | D.A.P.
75 Broad Street, Suite 630
New York, NY 10004
www.artbook.com

Distributed outside the United States and Canada by
Thames & Hudson
6-24 Britannia Street
London WC1X 9JD
www.thamesandhudson.com

Printed and bound in Turkey

PHOTOGRAPH CREDITS

In reproducing the images contained in this
publication, the Museum obtained the permission of
the rights holders whenever possible. If the Museum
could not locate the rights holders, notwithstanding
good-faith efforts, it requests that any contact
information concerning such rights holders be
forwarded so that they may be contacted for future
editions.

© ARCHI HATCH: p. 37 (both). Photograph by
The Asahi Shimbun via Getty Images: p. 21. © Kiyoshi
Awazu: p. 15. Digital Image © CNAC/MNAM, Dist.
RMN-Grand Palais/Art Resource, New York,
photograph by Jean-Claude Planchet: p. 11 (bottom).
© Yukio Futagawa / GA photographers: p. 10 (bottom).
Photograph *The Japan Architect*: p. 10 (top). © 2025
Kisho Kurokawa: p. 9. © Kisho Kurokawa Architect
and Associates (KKAA): pp. 16 (both), 17 (right), 26
(bottom), 27, 28–29. © Noritaka Minami: pp. 31, 38.
Digital Image © 2025 The Museum of Modern Art,
New York, Imaging and Visual Resources Department:
p. 10 (top); photograph by Robert Gerhardt: pp. 7, 9;
photograph by Jonathan Muzikar: pp. 2–3, 40–41,
inside back cover foldout (left); photograph by Martin
Parsekian: p. 15. Courtesy The Nakagin Capsule Tower
Restoration and Preservation Project: pp. 19 (both),
34–35, 39. Courtesy Chie Nomura: p. 36. © Tomio
Ohashi: pp. 5, 11 (top), 17 (left), 22, 23, 26 (top), 27,
inside back cover foldout (right), back cover.
© Jeremie Souteyrat: cover, p. 33 (both). © Taisei
Corporation: p. 25. Courtesy Kenjiro Ueda: p. 20.